Dear Family,

What's the best way to help your child love reading?

Find good books like this one to share—and read together!

Here are some tips.

- **Take a "picture walk."** Look at all the pictures before you read. Talk about what you see.

- **Take turns.** Read to your child. Ham it up! Use different voices for different characters, and read with feeling! Then listen as your child reads to you, or explains the story in his or her own words.

- **Point out words as you read.** Help your child notice how letters and sounds go together. Point out unusual or difficult words that your child might not know. Talk about those words and what they mean.

- **Ask questions.** Stop to ask questions as you read. For example: "What do you think will happen next?" "How would you feel if that happened to you?"

- **Read every day.** Good stories are worth reading more than once! Read signs, labels, and even cereal boxes with your child. Visit the library to take out more books. And look for other JUST FOR YOU! BOOKS you and your child can share!

The Editors

For George and Livvy   —BF

For Mom and Dad   —JK

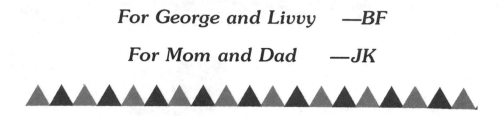

Text copyright © 2003 by Bernette Ford.
Illustrations copyright © 2003 by Jennifer Kindert.
Produced for Scholastic by COLOR-BRIDGE BOOKS, LLC, Brooklyn, NY
All rights reserved. Published by SCHOLASTIC INC.
JUST FOR YOU! is a trademark of Scholastic Inc.

ISBN 0-439-56849-8

14   12/0
Printed in the U.S.A   40
First Scholastic Printing, October 2003

Hurry Up!

by Bernette Ford

Illustrated by Jennifer Kindert

▲▲▲▲▲ JUST FOR YOU!™ ▲▲▲▲
▲▲ Level 1 ▲▲

Morning time...
Wake up.
Sit up.

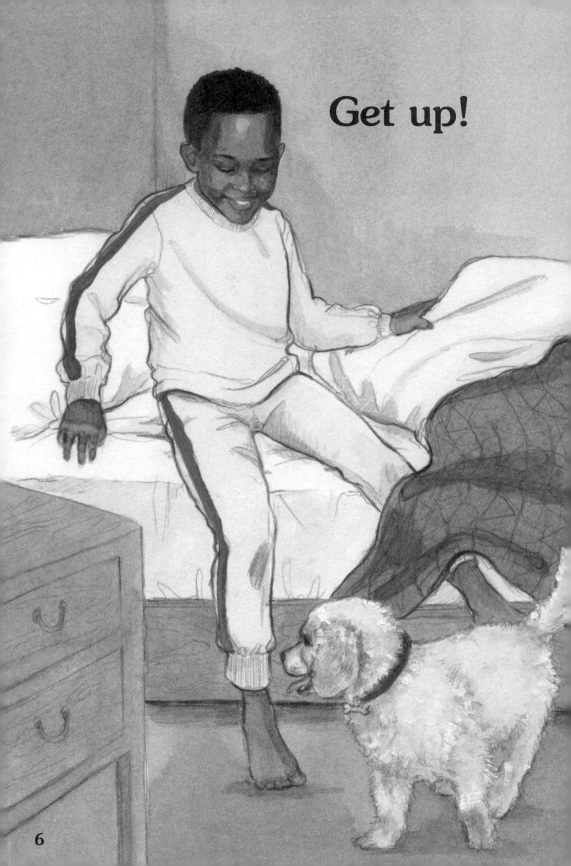

Get up!

Hurry up!
Wash up.

Button up.

Lace up.

Pack up.

Eat up.
Drink up.

Hurry up!

Line up!
Good-bye.

School time...
Hello Class!
Start up.

Add up.

2+3=5

Cut up.

PASTE UP

Finish up.
   Clean up.
Hurry up!

Play time...
Climb up.
Look up.

Look down.

Fall down!

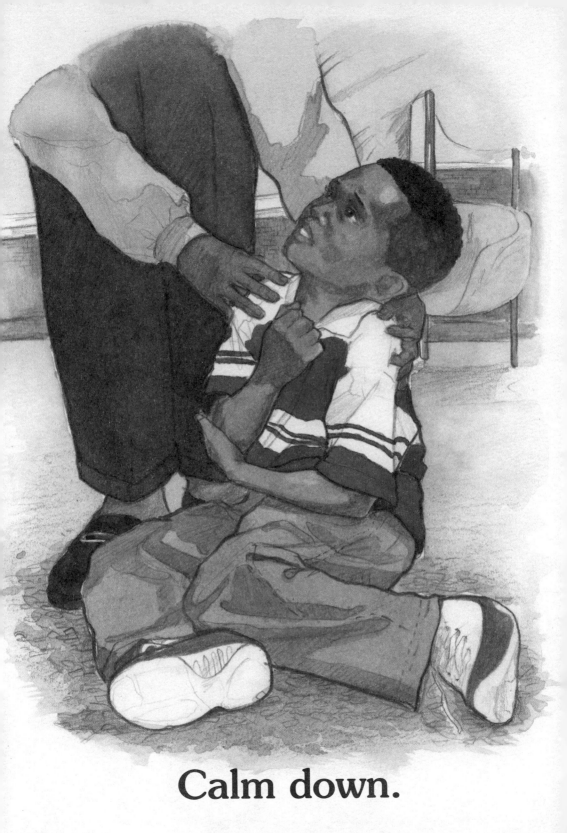

Calm down.

Slow down!
Time to go home.

Sit down.

Jump down.

Dinner time...
Chow down!

Knock down.
Slow down!

Bedtime...

Quiet down.

Lie down.
Sh-h-h-h-h!
Good night.

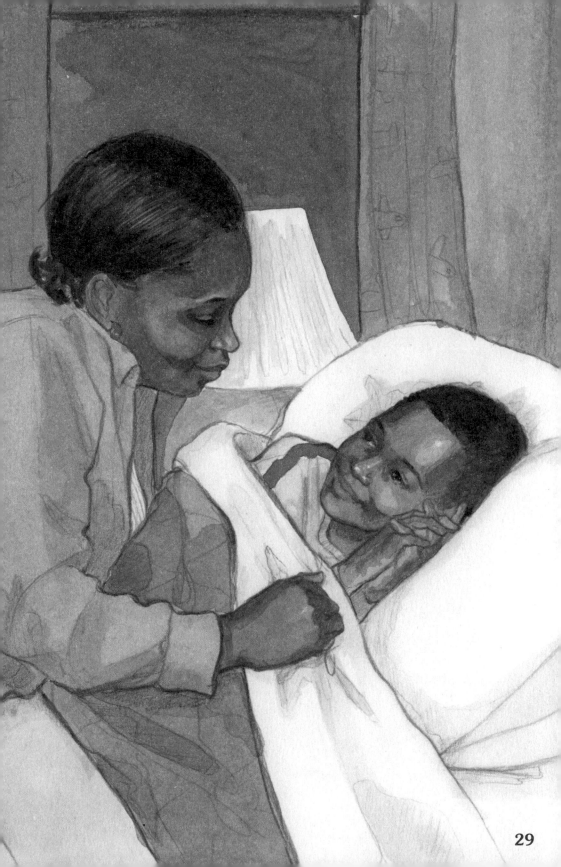

Here are some things for you to do.

All About YOU!

The boy in the story goes to school.
What does he do at school?
Tell about what YOU do at school.

How does the boy
get home from school?
Talk about how YOU get
to and from school.

The boy eats with his family.
Who are the people in his family?
Who are the people in YOUR family?

YOUR Puppy Story

The boy had a busy day.
What do you think his puppy
did all day?
Make up a new story.
Draw pictures, too.
This new story is written and
illustrated by YOU!

 TOGETHER TIME

*Make some time to share ideas about the story
with your young reader! Here are some activities
you can try. There are no right or wrong answers.*

Read It Again: Play this game as you read the
story aloud, with feeling! You read the beginning of
each sentence, then stop. Let your child finish each
sentence.

Act It Out: The author of the story uses the words
up and *down* in many ways. Together find your
favorite examples. Then act them out!

Think About It: Why did the boy have to hurry?
(There are several examples in the story.) Ask your
child, "Did anyone ever tell you to hurry up? How
did it make you feel?"

Meet the Author

BERNETTE FORD says, "My mom and dad read aloud to me from the time I was a baby. Maybe that's why I started reading before I went to kindergarten. I was writing my own stories and poems when I was in the first grade. I always had my head buried in a book. It was hard to pull me away from a good story! My mom was often telling me to hurry up! That's what I was thinking about when I got the idea to write this book."

Bernette grew up in Uniondale, New York, and graduated from Connecticut College. She worked as a children's book editor for many years. She works at home now, and has more time to do what she likes best—writing picture books! She is married to illustrator George Ford. They live in Brooklyn, New York, and they have one daughter—who also likes to read and write!

Meet the Artist

JENNIFER KINDERT says, "Ever since I was really little I wanted to be an artist when I grew up. *Hurry Up!* is only my second children's book. I had so much fun drawing and painting the little boy and his mom and sister. But the puppy was the most fun of all! I love all kinds of animals! This is a picture of me with a baby parrot named Jupiter.

Jennifer grew up in Sweden. She also lived in New York City for many years. She graduated from the Fashion Institute of Technology with a Fine Arts degree. She now lives in Dallas, Texas. She likes living there—most of the year, the weather is warmer than it is in New York or Sweden!